IMAGES
of America

THE
SACANDAGA
VALLEY

The old Fish House Covered Bridge, whose interior is shown above, is located over the Sacandaga River, in the town of Northampton in the Sacandaga Valley.

On the cover: This early stagecoach in front of the Northville House on North Main Street in the village of Northville is on its way north in 1895.

IMAGES
of America

THE
SACANDAGA
VALLEY

Randy Decker, Betty Tabor, and Jay Nellis

ARCADIA
PUBLISHING

Published by Arcadia Publishing
Charleston, South Carolina

Library of Congress Catalog Card Number: 99-069485

For all general information contact Arcadia Publishing at:
Telephone 843-853-2070
Fax 843-853-0044
E-mail sales@arcadiapublishing.com
For customer service and orders:
Toll-Free 1-888-313-2665

Visit us on the Internet at www.arcadiapublishing.com

Acknowledgments

This publication was made possible by the cooperation of three towns in the county of Fulton. The towns formed committees comprised of individuals who collected old photographs, selected the best ones, and compiled information about each of those chosen. Randy L. Decker, author of *The Fonda, Johnstown, & Gloversville Railroad,* shared photographs from his own collection for the Northampton chapter. Betty Tabor, town and village historian, worked with Joe and Joan Nehrbauer of the Mayfield Historical Society on the Mayfield chapter. Jay Nellis, town and village historian, worked with Broadalbin Historical Society members Mike and Audrey Taylor, Gordon Cornell, Stuart Hayes, Marty Clark, and Eliza Ammerall on the Broadalbin chapter. Lewis G. Decker, county historian, wrote the introduction and coordinated the project along with Lewis G. Decker Jr., deputy county historian.

CONTENTS

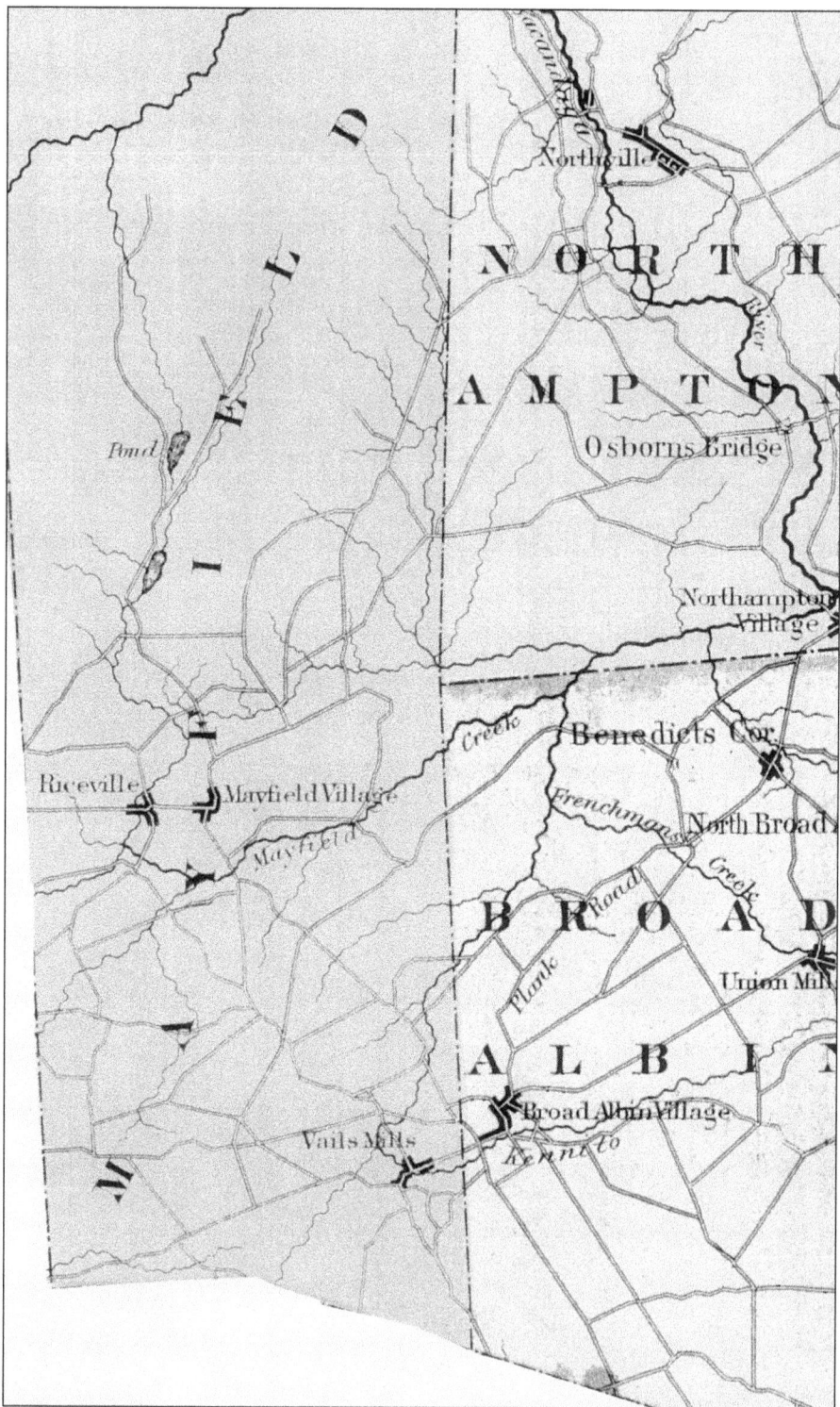

This 1868 map shows the three towns that make up Fulton County's portion of the Sacandaga Valley.

Introduction

The Sacandaga Valley, as it extends through Fulton County, contains three towns: the town of Northampton on its northern and eastern borders, the town of Mayfield on the northwestern side, and the town of Broadalbin in the southwestern portion. Today, this fertile valley with its farms and settlements has been flooded over and is now a large portion of the Great Sacandaga Lake.

In the forming of the Earth's surface, the heat and upheaval created mountain ranges. As the Earth cooled, glaciers advanced, gorging out valleys; as the glaciers receded, they deposited melted ice in these valleys, which formed early prehistoric lakes. The Sacandaga Valley was one of these early prehistoric lakes and through centuries of erosion, its banks were filled in. Once cleared, the valley afforded good river soil for farming. Three main rivers remained: the Sacandaga out of the north, the Vlaie, and the Kennyetto. Where they met, the lowland flooded in the spring. Its swale grass was a haven for breeding waterfowl and for producing fish and other wildlife in abundance.

Along this water route, Native Americans found easy access from the Mohawk Valley to the Hudson River and an ideal place to fish and hunt. One of the first recorded Europeans to have viewed this valley was Fr. Isaac Jogues. A Mohawk raiding party captured Jogues in the north and returned with him to the Mohawk Valley. In the *Jesuits Relations* journals, Jogues mentioned staying overnight among the huge pine trees on this water route before being brought to the village on the Mohawk the next day.

One of the first settlers in the Sacandaga Valley was Sir William Johnson. While residing at his second home at Fort Johnson, Johnson laid out a wagon road to the Sacandaga, blazing a tree every mile. He built a house on a high piece of ground where the Mayfield Creek entered the old Vlaie; this was his summer home, which he called Castle Cumberland. Later, he erected a camp, which he called the Fish House Lodge, near where the three streams emerged. Eventually, other settlers built here; today, the area still contains some of the valley's earliest homes.

Prior to the American Revolution, there were early settlements in the towns of Mayfield and Broadalbin. The Mayfield settlement was known as the Scots Settlement. The route from the Hudson to the Mohawk Valley remained a main line of travel and when the American Revolution occurred, continued to afford a route for raiding parties. A blockhouse was established and fortified to help prevent some of the raids coming from that direction. However, the Sacandaga Blockhouse ended up being of little value; it came under siege only on one occasion. That siege came one evening after the blockhouse had been abandoned and settler Solomon Woodworth had taken up residence there. A raiding party of a few Native Americans decided to burn the blockhouse down. Woodworth managed to hold off the raiders, who fled with their wounded comrades and were pursued the next day by the local militia.

Many settlers were not as fortunate as Woodworth; they ended up giving their lives or being held captive during these raids on the frontier. After the American Revolution, many more settlers arrived in the valley. They established villages where trades and factories prospered. The railroad was extended northward and in 1875, reached its northernmost terminal at Northville. The line went through the town of Mayfield and opened at Sacandaga Park, one of the state's best-known amusement centers and summer resorts. A few years later, a branch of the railroad reached the village of Broadalbin, affording freight and passenger service to the village.

The river now became a route to transport timber from the north to the many mills along its way, including those in Hadley, Luzerne, Corinth, and Glens Falls. Thousands of spectators lined the riverbanks each spring to watch the timber drives.

Everyone seemed to prosper up through the late 1920s. Then, the valley met its demise. Officials decided that the water flow had to be regulated to prevent the annual spring flooding of cities along the Hudson River, especially Cohoes and Albany. They chose to restrain the Sacandaga River by building a dam Conklingville. In 1930, the valley once again was flooded, as it had been in prehistoric days. It became a huge man-made lake, known today as the Great Sacandaga Lake. Although this lake provides some of the finest fishing and summer recreation in the East, it destroyed the many homes and farms and villages that were drowned under its waters. Through the years much of the valley's past history has been lost. We offer the early views in this book as one way of preserving some of the Sacandaga's past.

—Lewis G. Decker
Fulton County Historian

One

THE TOWN OF

BROADALBIN

Broadalbin was one of the first towns organized in Fulton County. It was formed from a portion of the old district of Caughnawaga on March 12, 1793, and was named by Daniel McIntyre after his native town in Scotland. Originally, the town included Northampton, which was removed in 1799, and the northeastern part of Perth, which was removed in 1842. Broadalbin is bordered by Northampton on the north, Saratoga on the east, Perth on the south, and Mayfield on the west.

The area, consisting of 24,104 acres, was known as Fonda's Bush until 1804, when a post office was established there. Residents of Scottish descent then secured the name of Broadalbin. In 1815, Dutch settlers unsuccessfully sought to incorporate the village under the name Rawsonville in honor of Dr. E.G. Rawson. No action was taken by the legislature, and the name never became permanent. Dr. Henry Finch, Benjamin Smith, and Cecil Finch, as well as many other prominent residents, actively advocated incorporation; Smith assisted in the completion of the necessary paperwork. The Village of Broadalbin was incorporated on August 8, 1924, and officials held their first meeting on September 28, 1924. Smith was elected the first president and during his first term, a new state law changed the title to mayor.

The first bus service from Amsterdam to Broadalbin started in 1912. Some village streets were paved by the 1920s, and the village waterworks was installed in 1927 with a water tower for pressure. Springs on South Second Avenue supplemented by deep water wells drilled into subterranean lakes below provided the water source. When this source began to dry up in the late 1960s, several new wells were drilled and found to be insufficient or low in water quality. Finally, a well with an excellent and ample supply was drilled on North Second Avenue.

The first village policeman was Frank Attey, followed by Herbert Morgan, Louis Savaccio, and Chester Burr. Broadalbin now employs deputy sheriffs to patrol and also utilizes the state police. The original village dump across from the Broadalbin-Mayfield cemetery was closed in 1948, and 25 acres of land on the Union Mills Road became the new dump site. That dump was closed after Broadalbin started using the county landfill and opened a transfer station. Broadalbin was an important part of the old Sacandaga Valley.

—Jay Nellis,
Town of Broadalbin Historian

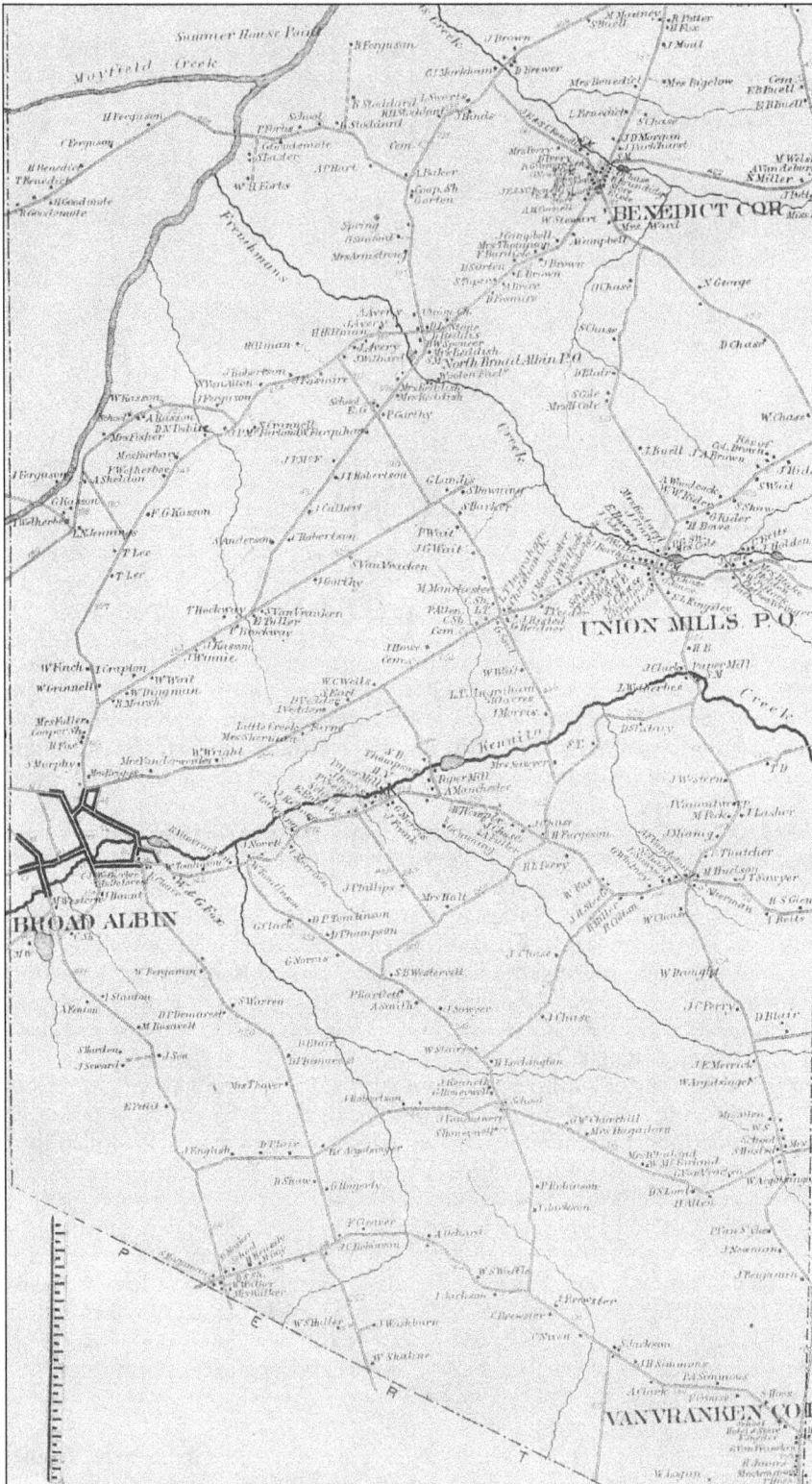

This map of the Town of Broadalbin is from 1868.

This photograph shows the Broadalbin High School basketball team of 1924-25.

The Broadalbin High School Class of 1926 can be seen in this photograph above. Located on School Street, the high school building is currently being used by the school district and the Board of Cooperative Educational Services for office and classroom space.

St. Joseph's Church, built in 1886 on Saratoga Avenue, was Broadalbin's first Catholic church. Father Sellman can be seen standing in the doorway.

The Kennyetto Volunteer Fire Company used this hand water pumper. The pumper was purchased on July 18, 1878, for $500.

This fire drill took place at what is now 19 School Street. The drill was conducted from the original volunteer firehouse.

The Broadalbin Coronet Band practices near the corner of West Main Street and First Avenue in Broadalbin, c. 1880s. This band was the predecessor of the Broadalbin Citizen's Band.

The Broadalbin High School cheerleaders, c. 1939, from left to right, are Edith Underwood, Bob McDade, Gladys Rockwell, Jeanette Brown, and Gordon Coloney.

The Husted Episcopal Chapel was built in 1888 by the Husted family for their own private use. The chapel was moved some 500 feet c. 1942, before it was torn down in April 1981.

The Husted family used this chapel privately on their estate on Maple Street.

This 1888 photograph of downtown Broadalbin shows an election banner hanging across the street. The stores shown in the background, from left to right, are Bradford and Dickinson with Mr. Dickinson in front of building, the Archibald Robertson store, A.H. Van Arnum Groceries, Paul Kissinger's Meat Market, and the American Hotel.

The Burr family sit in one of Broadalbin's first automobiles. Seen here, from left to right, are Howard Burr, Nelson Burr and his wife, Lillian Burr, and Mrs. Floyd Burr.

In this home lived Dr. William Chambers, father of author and illustrator Robert W. Chambers. The home was located to the right of what is currently St. Joseph's Church.

This group of men was involved in the construction of the Robert W. Chambers Mansion on North Street during the year 1912. Appearing in this photograph are George Lasher, Robert S. Waddell, William Dingman, Robert Earl, James Lasher, Arthur Sanford, Billy La Due, George Marple, Herb Lawton, William Gouley, Bill Williams, and Earl Ferguson.

James Shattuck owned and operated the Broadalbin–Amsterdam stage. This stage line was used for chartered and scheduled service; it remained active from 1911 to 1923.

The Earl Hotel, located on West Main Street, was named after its owner Melvin Earl. Earl purchased the building in 1848 and constructed an addition in 1882. This hotel was destroyed by fire on October 18, 1922.

Teacher Addie Pitcher is in the doorway of one of Broadalbin's one-room, rural schoolhouses.

This 1909 photograph shows Robert W. Chambers with his two hunting dogs. A renowned novelist and writer, Chambers had a summer home in Broadalbin.

19

The 1936 Broadalbin Central School faculty can be seen here, from left to right, as follows: (first row) Catherine Paris, Florence Jewel Jeffords, Dorothy Brown Stillman, Prof. Wilson Perkins, Catherine Suits, Anita Winne, and Arlene Dexter; (second row) William Stillman, Grace Lockyer, Anna George, Evelyn Elwood, Edith Rose Wood, Mary Hazard Sawyer, Helen Paris, Charlotte Davis Prussien, Dorothy Wemple Davis, and Clarence Heagle; (third row) Pauline Bartlett Stillman, Florence Dye, Mary Wolf, Letha Leslie, Theresa Sawyer Crannell, Dorothy Hathaway Reed, and Maymie McMann; (fourth row) Charlotte Hickans Groff, Rosealie Nellis, Hazel Rosa Luff, Charlotte Shattuck Leslie, Mae Halloran Hults, Fanny Greenslete, Vail Kelly, and Martha Wagner.

The old Chase Sawmill was located by the Maple Street Bridge in Broadalbin.

This photograph shows the rebuilding of the Broadalbin Knitting Mill after the original mills were destroyed by fire on November 29, 1905. This building later became the Mohawk Furniture Company, which was owned by Gem Crib and Crandel.

The Duane Howe Harness Shop was located on Thompson Street in Broadalbin.

Built c. 1885, the old church and parsonage at Benedicts Corner was destroyed by fire on November 15, 1945.

This photograph shows the Broadalbin Fife and Drum Corps. Pictured, from left to right, are Bill Moran, Arthur Weatherbee, Harry Gardner, Roy Vail, J. Mason, B. Jeans, and C. Howe.

The women employed at the Glove Shop at Benedicts Corner sewed cut leather into finished gloves. The men employed here cut the glove leather for the women to sew from size patterns.

The old Crossley Glove Company became known as the Korkay Chemical Company in later years. This building was demolished in 1997.

Construction on the original Fonda, Johnstown, & Gloversville Railroad depot in Broadalbin began in 1895 and was completed in 1896.

The original depot on the Fonda, Johnstown, & Gloversville line at Broadalbin was later replaced, using the same structure that is shown here. The building was abandoned when the train ceased to run here. Today, it serves as an antique shop.

The tracks shown in the foreground lead to the Fonda, Johnstown, & Gloversville Railroad. The Broadalbin depot can be seen in the background.

The old Kunjamuck Hall was built in 1893 for the International Order of the Redmen, Kunjamuck Tribe No. 187, which was newly formed in the village. The hall was used for the group's meetings.

The Kennyetto Fire Company drill team can be seen in front of the Union Free School in the village of Broadalbin.

This photograph shows a village block dance under way on Main Street in Broadalbin.

Dr. Henry Finch lived on North Main Street, just above the business district in the village of Broadalbin, *c*. the 1920s.

This 1925 Model T Ford belonged to Eliza Cloutier, who taught at the the Kasson Street Schoolhouse from 1926 to 1927. The school now lies under the waters of the Great Sacandaga Lake.

This scene of destruction shows all that remained of the Broadalbin Knitting Mill after a disastrous fire occurred on November 29, 1905.

This photograph shows a group of men laying the water main from Glen Wild for the Amsterdam waterworks.

The old American Hotel on Main Street was purchased and torn down by Kitty Husted to help widen Main Street.

Warden Potter was the local store manager of the Grand Union Super-ette on North Main Street in Broadalbin, c. the late 1940s.

The old Kennyetto Inn on West Main Street is in existence today as the Hotel Broadalbin.

Broadalbin, N. Y. Suspension Bridge.

Kitty Husted built this old swinging bridge in 1890 to create a shortcut from the Maple Street neighborhood to the knitting mill and the downtown area.

This photograph shows the swinging bridge after it was destroyed by an ice jam in 1936.

Built in 1886, the old St. Joseph's Catholic Church was located on Saratoga Avenue. Before this building was erected, Mass was conducted at the old Tom Warren home, as well as at the homes of other parishioners.

The factory of Dye & Robertson Glove Manufacturers was located on School Street until January 9, 1909, when it was destroyed by fire.

South Main St. Broadalbin, N. Y.

This view of West Main Street, Broadalbin, was taken looking west.

Henry Hillman and Edward Johnson stand behind the counter of their hardware store in this photograph, taken in 1924.

This photograph of the Broadalbin Knitting Company Mill was photographed prior to the November 29, 1905 fire.

The Kennyetto Fire Company had a Reo Speed Wagon with a Child's fire body that originally cost $4,000. The fire truck arrived in Broadalbin on December 22, 1923. Pictured on the truck, from left to right, are George Farley III, George Farley Sr., George English, William Summers, Wesley Kelley, and John Kelley.

A load of Trevetts rocking chairs travel en route to local stores. Trevetts chairs could be identified by the special finials that were carved on each piece.

This Broadalbin Boy Scout troop is encamped at Spy Lake.

This photograph was taken in front of Burr's Store on North Main Street, Broadalbin, before the downtown fire of January 28, 1914.

The Robert W. Chambers Mansion is now used as a residence for the priest of St. Joseph's Catholic Church.

This old rural, one-room schoolhouse was located at Gortley Corners in Broadalbin.

Glove cutters and workers can be seen in an interior view of one of Broadalbin's glove shops. The glove cutters, using different sized patterns, cut the leather for the sewers to finish into gloves.

In this interior view of one of Broadalbin's glove shops, workers sew gloves and prepare them for distribution. Glove making and leather processing was Fulton County's main industry; every community in the county had something to do with the trade.

Broadalbin Civil War veterans line up for a village parade near the bandstand in the little park. Today, a monument stands at the intersection of West Main, North Main, and Bridge Streets.

Schoolchildren stop to have their picture taken in front the F. Gulick Harness Shop.

Destroyed by fire in 1905, the Eli Stockwell House is shown here after it was rebuilt.

Taken sometime prior to 1947, this photograph shows the home of Gordon "Buckey" Weaver, located on the Stevers Mills Road (old Route 29).

This early winter scene was photographed in Benedict in the town of Broadalbin.

The Willing Workers Sunday school class of the Broadalbin Methodist Church presents a minstrel show in 1941. Appearing on stage are Clara Christopher, Edith Reinhardt, Louise Hohler Burr, Beulah Kane, Reverend Spear, Gertrude Sawyer, Dorothy Crannell, and Grace Smarup.

Mr. Fish can be seen on his horse-drawn lawn mower; he used to mow and keep up the grounds of the Husted Estate in Broadalbin.

Students pose in front of one of the town of Broadalbin's rural, one-room schoolhouses. Before the town's schools were consolidated, Broadalbin had more than a dozen such one-room schoolhouses and districts. Many of these structures are gone today.

Mills Corners School was located on Route 29 East near the current-day Flea Hill in the town of Broadalbin. At one time, Mills Corners had its own post office; today, mail comes through the post office in Broadalbin.

Miss M. K. Husted's Residence and Italian Gardens, Broadalbin, N. Y.

This view shows the Italian gardens on the Husted Estate. The Kitty Husted residence can be seen in the background at the left.

This view shows an early Broadalbin baseball team.

"THE CITIZEN'S BAND" BROADALBIN, N. Y.

Members of the Broadalbin Citizen's Band pose in front of the old Union Free School, which was built in 1895.

46

Members of the Broadalbin High School Class of 1934, from right to left, are as follows: (front row) Pauline Anderson, Hazel Phillips, Elizabeth Bartlett, Elma Finch, Sonia Sirotick, Carol Fraker, Thelma Mac Vean, and Irene Skapik; (back row) Howard Weiderman, Stanton Sabattis, Geneva White, George Kross, Marianne Seward, Schyler Lathers, Kathleen Swears, Harold Eaton, Norma Phillips, Andre Beletsky, and Arthur Frank. This class was the last to graduate from the high school on School Street.

Located on School Street, the Union Free School taught grades 1 through 12. The building was constructed in 1924 and used until 1931, when it was replaced with a new three-story school.

Robert W. Chambers stands outside the house on Maple Street that served as his summer residence until he built the Chambers Mansion.

Two

THE TOWN OF MAYFIELD

On April 1, 1794, several men gathered in a crude log church on the Nine Mile Tree Road and elected officers to conduct business for the Town on Mayfield. The town was formed, and it was named after a Mayfield patent granted in 1770. It was one of the first towns created in the town of Fulton. Selah Woodworth was the first owner of land, purchased from Sir William Johnson.

Situated in the foothills of the Adirondack Mountains, Mayfield is comprised of rolling hills, which in the early years had an abundant supply of grain fields for farming, several limestone quarries, and an abundance of trees for lumbering. Because of the many streams flowing into Mayfield, there were gristmills, tanneries, and sawmills. Mayfield's hamlets include Riceville, Wilkins Corners, Vail Mills, Woods Hollow, Munsonville, Jackson Summit, Shawville, Closeville, Anthonyville, and Red Bunch. Mayfield was built around the tannery and glove business; the area had an abundance of hemlock trees, the bark of which was used in the tanning process.

At least 15 burying grounds existed in Mayfield, all of which have been recorded. The town has had many churches, including the very old Central Presbyterian Church and the United Methodist Church, which are still active today. At one time, the Quakers were also a well-represented group in the area.

Mayfield had 17 schools, the first being a German one. All of the schools have now been consolidated into one large high school, located on School Street, and one elementary school, located on North Main Street. Both rank high in the area as instructional facilities.

The village was incorporated in 1896. The fire department was incorporated more than 100 years ago, with the first firehouse located on School Street. Now on North School Street, the department recently acquired a modern building with grounds that will allow for expansion.

By 1820, the town's population was 376; by 1840, it was 2,615; today, it stand at about 7,000. Mayfield can boast about its history, as it has more historical markers than any other locality. The Mayfield historian and the historical society are continuously working to preserve the town's heritage.

Although Mayfield has only a few stores left, the town will stay alive. No matter what the cause, the people of Mayfield have always pushed forward, worked hard, and joined together. That is why Mayfield is nicknamed Bannertown—for its many celebrations and parades with banners stretched across the streets.

—Betty Tabor
Mayfield Town Historian

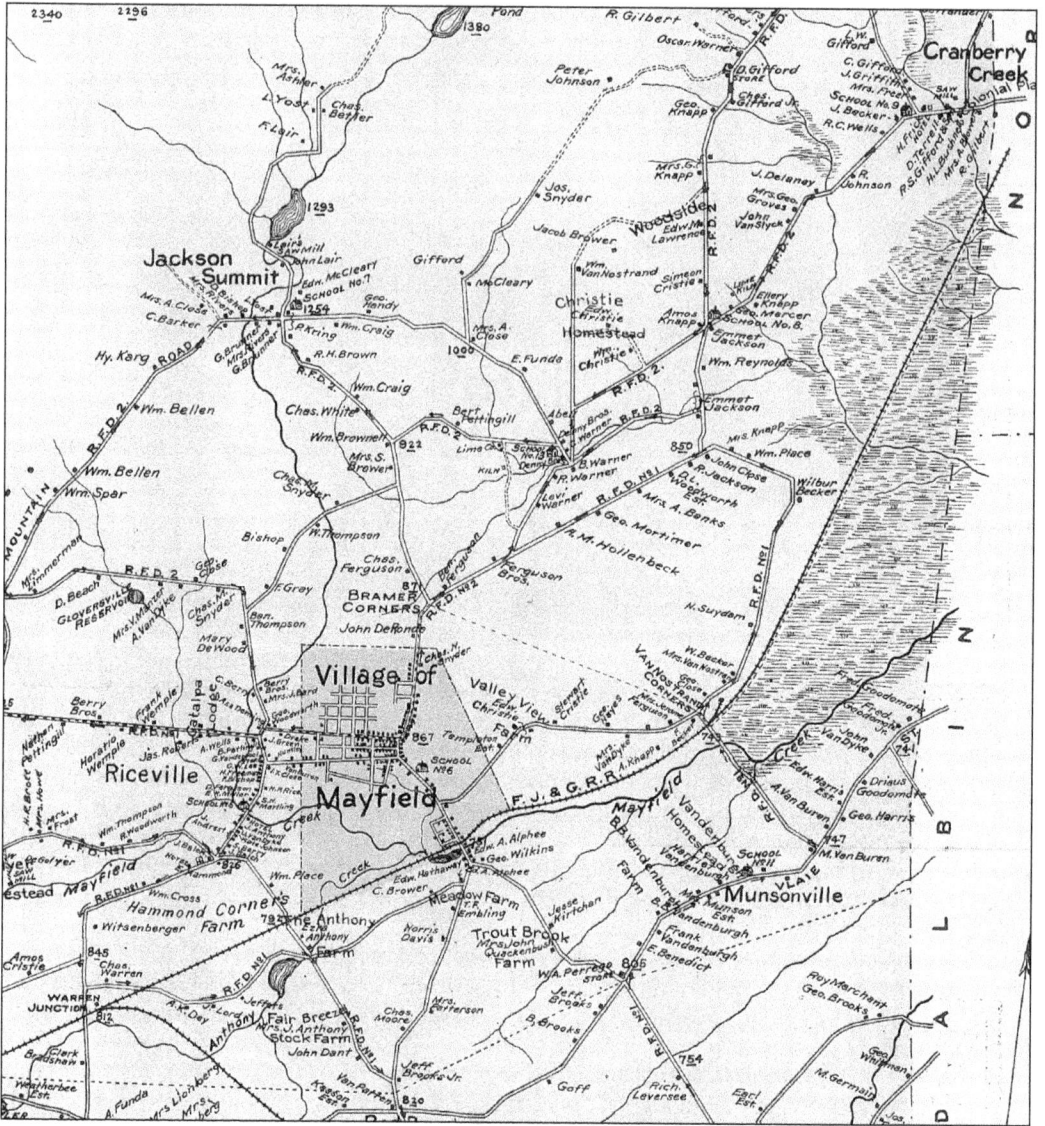

This early map shows Mayfield before the Great Sacandaga Lake was created.

Oliver Rice can be seen with his daughter-in-law Harriet Cozzens. Rice is one of the notable residents of Mayfield. He was born in 1764 and died in 1859. He was a Revolutionary War soldier and a businessman. He built a clothier's mill in 1795 on the bank of the Mayfield Creek. He ran this business until about 1830. The small hamlet in the western part of Mayfield was named Riceville in his honor. In the early 1800s, he built the Rice Homestead, which is currently the home of the Mayfield Historical Society.

Lucius Rice I, the son of Oliver Rice, poses in front of the Rice Homestead. He was born in 1807 and died in 1861, barely outliving his father.

Many events are held throughout the year on the grounds of the Rice Homestead—the most popular being the annual Christmas open house.

The square in the center of Mayfield appeared this way c. the late 1800s. Prominent businesses included Browns Drug Store, Hartin Dry Goods, and Hartin Grocery Store. The two houses on the left were moved in later years when North School Street was constructed; they are now occupied by the Scotts and Dugans.

The Jackson House was located in the middle of the village. Lila Wilkins sits on the porch; her father was the proprietor. The building burned down in 1886.

These ruins of the famous Jackson House were photographed following the disastrous fire in 1886. The area was rebuilt soon thereafter. In the background at the left is the Methodist Episcopal Church.

Mr. Blaha's Riceville Hotel, located on Riceville Road, was very popular in its day. Part of it burned and was later turned into a house. This photograph was taken c. 1915. A garage has since been added to the property, which is now owned by Riceville Auto.

This photograph shows an early-1900s cutter in front of the Mayfield Glove Company, with the Methodist church at the right.

This sleigh on North Main Street is heading west toward the School Street intersection, which was Route 30 at that time. The second building on left was owned by the Titcombs; it later became Ellithorpes Market.

The Bellen House was located on Jackson Summit. Appearing in this *c.* 1884 photograph are Civil War veteran Elmer William Tell, Mary C. Frederick, and William Bellen. This house is now owned by Jim and Karen Rulison.

Delbert Wemple poses in his Riceville grocery store. The market burned in 1938; it was rebuilt near the same area and was operated for many years by the Wemples. The original building had been used for nearly 100 years.

The Goodemote home was located on the end of Vandenburgh Point in the Munsonville area; it was taken down when the Sacandaga Lake was formed. The dark gray house was photographed in the early 1900s. The women sitting out front are Ada Griffis and Esther Moore, the mother of Ruth Phillips.

Harold Johnson, on the right, and possibly Harold McGillery are pictured in this *c.* 1910 view of Sacandaga Park.

Rowen H. Brown owned the Meat Market on Wheels. He was the butcher and the cutter. He packaged and delivered the meat from his Second Avenue house to private homes.

This interior of the Mayfield Grill on School Street was photographed shortly after Prohibition ended. The Jerome Theater, which opened above the grill in 1927, provided movies and live piano music before the show. The grill is still in operation. Almost everyone remembers Juley and Sophie and Al and Jen.

The Mayfield Garage was located at 20 West Main Street in 1928. Ernest Kuhne was the proprietor. The garage was previously operated by William Mason. This site is now part of the old Coleco plant parking lot.

This view of the T.E. Embling Store on South School Street was taken in the early 1900s. Embling, who came from England, ran a very successful business for many years. The building is currently the home of the Mayfield Servicemen's Club.

The Harlan Brown Ice-cream Parlour was located in the village square in the early 1940s. Patrons in the picture include Joan Johnson (Bennett), Bernard Wemple, Bruce Wemple, Blanche Marcellus (Auriemma), Harry Fowler, and Harlan Brown.

This late-18th-century Greek Revival-style home was reportedly part of the Underground Railroad. The most notable resident was abolitionist and community activist Capt. William Shaw of the Civil War. The area was called Shawville after his death. One slave, who was brought to freedom by the captain, remained in the area until his death in the mid-1900s. The home is currently owned by Joan and Joe Nehrbauer.

The Mayfield Diner was located on North Main Street and was operated by various people, including Evelyn Bennett. Pictured in this early-1940s photograph, from left to right, are Hugh Donlon, Bob Donlon, George Oathout, and Harold Richardson. The diner was town down in the late 1950s.

The little post office was located in the village square for many years until it was destroyed by fire in 1971. The post office's temporary site on Route 30 became its permanent site. Many residents felt the move of the post office altered the atmosphere of the village.

Samuel A. Gilbert settled and named Cranberry Creek. Born in 1790, Gilbert built the first house in Cranberry Creek; the house still stands.

Abigail Gilbert, the wife of Samuel Gilbert, was born in 1782. Agnes Gilbert, who currently lives in Cranberry Creek, is the great great-granddaughter of Samuel and Abigail Gilbert. Sylvia Parker, Agnes Gilbert's daughter, is the next generation.

The Gilbert House can be seen on the left. The Fonda, Johnstown, & Gloversville train crossing is on the far side of this house. The house was moved, and Sylvia Parker now lives there and uses the carriage house as her garage. The Great Sacandaga Lake now covers the area where the house originally stood.

This Cranberry Creek church was built in the mid-1800s. It was an ideal stopping-off place midway between Mayfield and Northville during stagecoach days. Later, the church was moved to Gilbert Road. It was demolished in the 1980s, following a slight disaster in which the floor caved in during an Easter Sunday service. A new church was built to replace it.

Andrew Yorks of Jackson Summit is seen here, busily engaged in his work. For years, Yorks produced wooden grain shovels, yokes to carry water, and butter paddles.

Members of the 1910 Mayfield Fire Department, from left to right, are as follows: (front row) Walt Olson, Ed Delaney, Roy Wemple, Frank Newton, Charles Reynolds, Elmer Wheeler, Earl Day, and Andrew Beach; (back row) Octavio King, Jerome Becker, James Davidson, Henry Besaw, Vean White, Bert Seney, Frank Bennett, William Cooley, and Truman Donlon.

The Mayfield Fire Department purchased the latest in firefighting pumpers in 1922.

The Mayfield Fire Department hose cart, named Yellow Kid, was built by Joe Bennett in 1895 for $31.25. Now painted red, the cart has been preserved and stored at the firehouse and is used today in parades and for exhibition.

The Mayfield Railroad Station in Shawville is now underwater. The Fonda, Johnstown, & Gloversville Railroad was used not only for passenger service but also for shipping from Mayfield; a popular destination was the Sacandaga Park. Byron Griffis, the father of DeWitt Griffis, was the conductor.

Myron Gilbert was the station agent at the Cranberry Creek Railway Station.

This house on Wilkins Corners (now Phelps Street) in Riceville belonged to John Wilkins and his wife, seen here, *c.* 1893. The house still stands and is now the home of Lee Eschler.

This train wreck occurred in front of the Mayfield Station in Shawville on August 22, 1903. When the water level is down, remnants of the station can be seen, including the tracks, which are covered by a section of the Little Mayfield Lake.

The James E. Kelly Glove Company was later operated by Bennett and then Wilkins. It was located on the corner of Second Avenue and School Street. The building was torn down in the 1960s.

The Amos Christie Glove Shop, photographed c. 1896, was known for many years as the Close and Christie Glove Company. When Amos Christie disposed of his interests, the name was changed to the Mayfield Glove Company.

The following women can be seen in this 1940s picture of the Wilkins Glove Shop, from left to right, Irma Lindsley, Alice Parker, Mildred Herrick, Edith Warner, and Abbie Hopkins.

The Dixon Glove Company took part this early-1940s parade. Parades were held to mark the beginning of Old Home Days in Mayfield.

The Mayfield Glove Company, built in 1889, was erected on the site of the Jackson House, which had been destroyed three years earlier by fire. Following the demise of the glove industry in Mayfield, the building was used as an apartment house until it was destroyed by fire in 1986.

This Mayfield Glove Company float appeared in an early-1940s Mayfield Servicemen Club parade. The glove shop is on the left.

This image of the cutting room in the Wilkins Glove Shop is presumed to be from the early 1900s. Photographs of glove shop interiors are rare.

The Ed Christie Shop and the Van Burens Shop were located on West Main Street. Van Burens was lost to a fire in 1922. The Christie shop today is part of the original Coleco factory. Margie Stewart worked there in 1922; born on April 27, 1906, she sewed gloves at the Mayfield Glove Shop for more than 35 years before retiring at the age of 71.

Only men appear in this early-1900s photograph of the Wilkins Glove Shop. Possibly, the image was taken before the time that women were employed at the company.

This rare photograph of the Riceville Tannery on the Rice property was taken in 1899. The tannery was located on the Mayfield Creek. Workers appearing in photograph include Silos Ferguson, Will Stliff, Ed Christie, Dan Ferguson, Billy Peek, Francis Wells, Henry Deming, Friday Sweet, ? Demming, Lewis Pluss, Frank Newton, Chris Olson, and ? Pettingill.

The North Main Street School No. 6, seen here in 1870, was built ten years earlier and was known as the Union Free School until the new one was built on School Street. After the closing of the school, many business ventures were carried on here; in the early 1950s, Dr. Horenstein opened his medical practice here.

The Union Free School on School Street was built in the late 1800s and closed in 1939; it housed grades one through eight. The school bell is on display at the Rice Homestead.

Through the efforts of Dick Stewart and a few friends, the school bell from the Union Free School, built in 1890, was saved from the demolition crew. The bell was stored in the present school until 1997, at which time it was carefully moved to the Rice Homestead, where it is on display.

This unique photograph shows the School Street Union Free School, on the right, built in 1890, and the present Mayfield High School completed in 1939, which included kindergarten through grade 12. The high school has had a few additions and now contains grades 7 through 12. The elementary school is located on North Main Street.

This 1913 photograph shows one of the smallest schoolhouses that exited in the area during the time when country schools were prevalent. Built in 1868 by Thomas Weatherbee, the Woods Hollow School was overtaken by the flooding of Sacandaga Lake in 1928. The pupils then went to Broadalbin.

Teachers at the Cranberry Creek School in 1916 were Adeline Albro and Miriam Gorthey, who later lived in a two-family house on 30 West Main Street.

The Jackson Summit School No. 7, rebuilt after the first one burned in 1865, was used until 1939. It was the largest school in the district, having eight grades. Converted into a home by Garth and Judy Wemple, it is presently the Hannis residence.

Unknown pupils pose on the fence of the Foote District School, c. the early 1920s. Notice the girls' high top shoes. The school is located on Route 146, which is also known as the Farm-to-Market Road.

Seen at Munsonville School on November 12, 1916, from left to right, are Hene Winnie (Brower), Jenne Fox, Tom Johnson, Scott VanDenburgh, and teacher Mildred Benedict.

This photograph shows students of the Careys Corners School, c. 1913–1914. Some of the students are Gladwin Jackson, Jerome Becker, Owen Knapp, Nathan Brower, Dwella Knapp, Grant Manzor, Ruth Johnson, teacher Pearl Conklin, Royal Knapp, Seward Brower, Peter Johnson, Dorothy Knapp, Margie Becker (Stewart), and Ella Warner.

Pupils pose on the front steps of Franks Corner School, c. 1932–1935. The school, located on the end of Progress Road and Route 29, educated students up through the sixth grade, who afterward went on to Broadalbin.

These students attended the Jackson Summit School. From left to right, they are as follows: (front row) Warren "Buster" Van Derwerker and Freeman Yorks; (middle row) Robert Peck, Rebecca DeVoe, Minnie Van Derwerker, and Ethelinda DeVoe; (back row) Francis DeVoe.

Organized in 1785, the Methodist Episcopal Church appears here before major structural changes took place on the interior. The appearance of the outside has changed very little over the years. The inside still has a balcony. Today, it is known as the United Methodist Church.

M.E. CHURCH,

The Central Presbyterian Church on North Main Street was built in 1823. Changes have been made inside and an addition constructed on the back; however, the appearance of the church has remained much the same. Notice the gaslamp and the plank sidewalk.

This *c.* 1930s image of the Odd Fellows Lodge shows, from left to right, as follows: (front row) Joe Bennett, Ivan Wemple, and Baltus Dixon; (Back row) Oliver Van Buren, Bob Groves, Edmond Delaney, Willis Warner, Roy Wemple, Delbert Wemple, and Harvey Newton.

The old Gifford Sawmill at Cranberry Creek can be seen with the old Stone Arched Bridge in the foreground.

This Mayfield Grange Hall was built in 1931 on Phelps Street. The grange's original site, across from the Mayfield Railroad Station, is now underwater.

Bill Whitman is in the center back row at the Mayfield Grange, *c.* 1945. The Mayfield Grange was formed and chartered in 1890.

The Vail Mills buildings included a grain mill. A millpond dam was used to hold back water to run the waterwheel. The pond is still there. Mr. Vail and his mill later gave the settlement the name Vail Mills.

The beautiful Nathan Van Denburgh Farm, which was located in Munsonville in the 1920s, is now underwater.

Cynthia Nickloy, a midget from Mayfield, worked for the Ringling Brothers Circus and was also a munchkin in *The Wizard of Oz*. Known as Princess Marguerite, she was a member of the Methodist Episcopal Church.

Some of Mayfield's World War I veterans can be seen with their girlfriends or wives.

The Getman Memorial in the Union Free Cemetery was dedicated by the Getman family in 1916 to Capt. David G. Getman Jr. and members of his regiment, Company I, 10th N. Y. Cavalry, who are listed on the monument. It is the only sculpture in the Mayfield cemetery and will be included in the Save Outdoor Sculptures by the National Institute for the Conservation of Cultural Property.

Erected in 1776, the Dunham House on Paradise Point Road burned down and was later rebuilt. It has a historical marker stating that a Native American raid took place there; Jacob Dunham and his son Samuel were killed in April 1779. Other family members escaped by hiding in nearby woods.

Located in Riceville, the Arch Tabor Taxidermist shop was built in the late 1920s and operated for more than 40 years. The business changed hands over the year and is still in existence.

Theron Brooks can be seen on the latest pickup truck of the day, believed to be an early Model T Ford, at Brooks Farm on the Vandenburgh Point Road.

The Mayfield Fire Company gives young people rides in the fire truck during one of Mayfield's annual Old Home Day celebrations. Visible are Hisert's Drug and Soda Fountain and the This and That Store next door.

The Mayfield baseball team, *c.* pre-1887, from left to right, are Henry Hartin, Baltus Dixon, DeWitt Hartin, William Thompson, Merl Haines, Simeon Christie, Frank Goodemote, John Roberts, and Mac Danforth.

Members of the Mayfield baseball team of 1894 are as follows: (front row) Ernest Wilkins and Friday Chapman with one unidentified player; from left to right, (middle row) Joe Bennett, Louie Jerome, Ralph Dingman, Frank "Bob" Warner, and Frank "Fat" Warner; (back row) Jim Hickey, Roy Wilkins, Harry Zimmerman, Emery Tyler, and Willard "Dizzy Day" DeGraff.

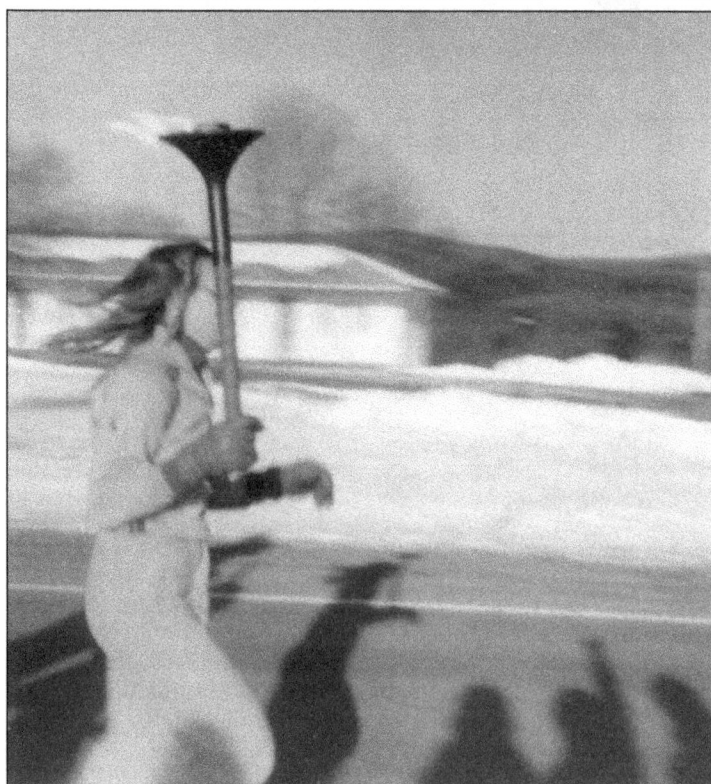

Another great Mayfield baseball team, the Mayfield Tigers, can be seen, from right to left, as follows: (front row) Nelson Wilkins; (middle row) Rufe Gifford, UtyEutemark,DizzyDeGraff, Bunnie Bellen, Rat Martling, and Johnnie Gifford; (back row) Prof. McCausland, Kee Kasajir, Squaker LaRowe, Harv Richardson, Ray Carramore, and Pickles O'Brien.

The Olympic torch went through Mayfield on the way to Lake Placid. Speical events were held in Mayfield on February 7, 1980. Many local people joined the runner and ran for several miles.

Three

THE TOWN OF
NORTHAMPTON

The town of Northampton, located in the northeastern portion of Fulton County, covers just over 22,000 acres. Northampton derived its name from a 6,000-acre land patent of the same name granted by King George II in 1741. The town of Northampton was officially created in 1799 through a subdivision of the town of Broadalbin.

Unquestionably, the most defining feature of this picturesque town are the waters of the Sacandaga River. Since the last Ice Age, these waters have flowed from the Adirondack Mountains into the large fertile valley called Sacandaga by the Native Americans, continuing on to the southern end of the town and turning to the northeast, following its course to merge with the Hudson River. Long before recorded history, this river way and its valley were well known to the Native Americans for fishing and hunting.

With the arrival of the white man, the valley's fertile soil was used for farming and the river was used extensively for industry and the transportation of Adirondack timber headed for the paper mills and sawmills established throughout the Hudson Valley. Northampton's villages and settlements were a direct result of these industries, and people settled here by the thousands. By the 1870s, a railroad was built that reached the outskirts of the large village of Northville. This new form of transportation carried timber, manufactured products, and the people who lived or worked here; it also carried the many summer religious groups, known as the Adirondack Conference, who had been traveling to this area for several years to enjoy its peaceful beauty.

With the introduction of the railroad, the town continued to grow. A beautiful park was created near Northville, appropriately called Sacandaga Park, bringing tens of thousands of summer visitors to the area. Many large hotels and businesses were built to cater to the visitors' needs. Northampton enjoyed this period of growth and prosperity until the latter half of the Roaring Twenties.

Extensive flooding each spring along the Sacandaga River, along the Hudson River, and in the capital city of Albany created the need to better regulate the Hudson River. The solution was not looked upon with enthusiasm by the people of Northampton or the surrounding areas. By 1930, a dam was to be completed at Conklingville, located at the northeastern end of the valley. Everything in the valley—villages, homes, farmlands, cemeteries, factories, covered bridges, roads, forests, railroads—had to be either moved or destroyed, as the river itself was to cover almost half of the town under the newly formed Sacandaga Reservoir. Many local families remember this sad event and speak of the constant smoke that filled the valley as construction continued at Conklingville.

Today, the renamed Great Sacandaga Lake brings a new beauty to Northampton. Many camps and homes have been built along its massive shoreline. Boating, fishing, swimming, marinas, bait shops, and beaches have replaced many of the attractions and businesses that once made this area a summer mecca. Northampton's inhabitants share their memories of the valley, and their history has been diligently preserved by many past and present historians for everyone's use in the future. Many of the photographs used in this book were taken by persons unknown who had the foresight to preserve them and the generosity to share them with us all.

—Randy L. Decker

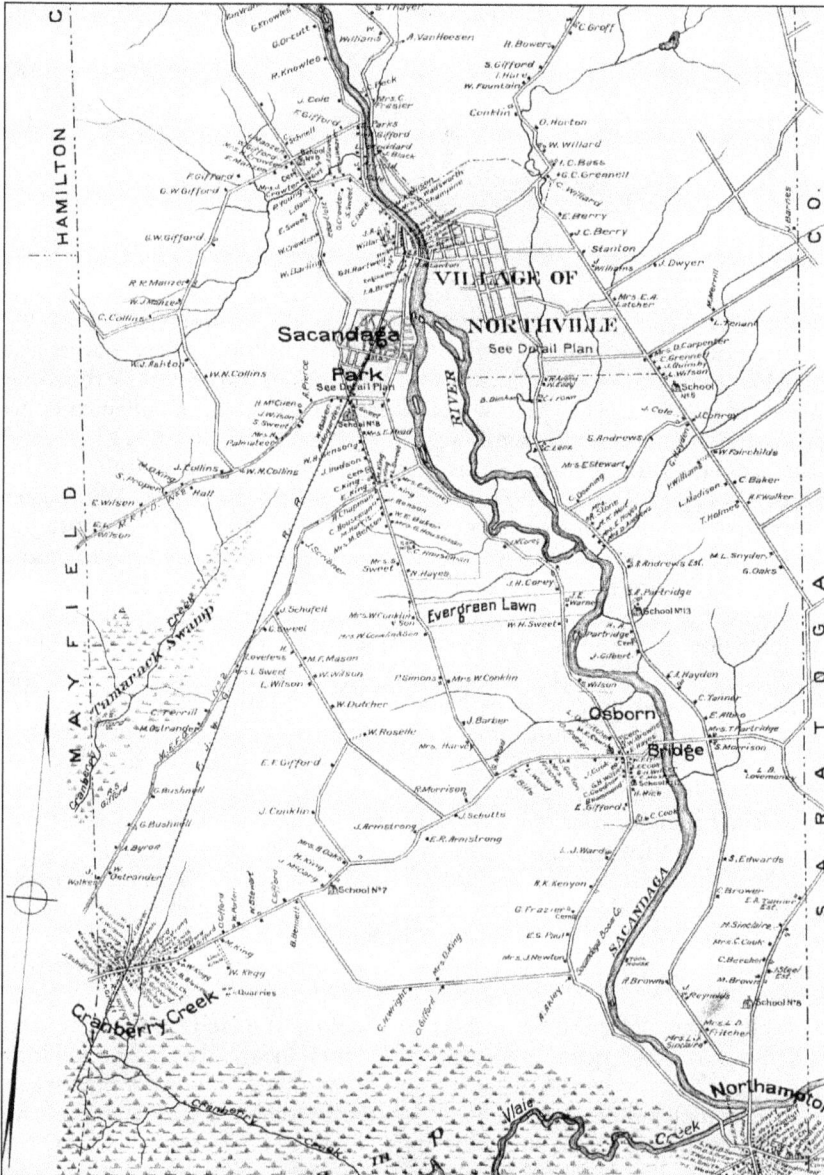

This map of the town of Northampton came from the *New Century Atlas of Montgomery and Fulton Counties, N.Y.*, printed by the Century Map Company in 1905.

The animal in the foreground seems mildly interested as an early photographer captures a view of Parkville in the distance. This small but industrious settlement grew around several mills that were located by a small dam and bridge constructed across the Sacandaga River about one mile upstream from the bridge at Northville. The dam was built in the late 1820s by Andrew Mcnutt, who had settled here from Scotland sometime before 1800. A small tannery, constructed in the early 1850s, called the Park Tannery, gave the community its name. This village grew to a significant size and was later incorporated into the village of Northville. Several homes were moved from this community before it was destroyed by the arrival of the lake. This photograph was taken at the end of Prospect Street in the village of Northville, looking northwest.

This winter view shows the community of Parkville.

Colonel Hartwood, in similar fashion to Theodore Roosevelt, sports his Spanish-American War uniform on a bear-hunting trip in Vean Sweet Clearing, near the end of the 19th century. Mr. Sweet is on the left and Mr. Gifford from nearby Johnny Cake Hollow (later renamed Gifford's Valley) is in the center.

The Little Red Schoolhouse, a one-room country school, was located on the southeast corner of the Collins-Gifford Road and High Rock Road intersection in Giffords Valley. Today, this small school has been moved inside the village of Northville to South Main Street and has been diligently filled with local memorabilia for the Northville-Northampton Museum.

Located across the river from Northville just south of the bridge and along the road to Sacandaga Park, the Ralph Giffords General Store was a favorite stop for many young Northvillians, who often walked to the nearby park. Giffords store was washed downstream during a flood that occurred in March 1929.

This photograph, taken looking north, shows the east side of Main Street in Northville's early business district. The season appears to be late fall; people are lining up in front of the R.G. Dewitt & Company 5 & 10 and 25¢ store for what must have been a very good sale. The Kested and Bowman Drug and Cigar Store is directly behind the blanketed horse in the foreground. Competition in Northville is evident from the Copeland and Skinner Drugstore and Ice-cream Shop, located on the north side of the R.G. Dewitt & Company Store. Just down the street are the barber poles of the shop located on the second floor of a small wooden building, built c. 1860s.

This bird's-eye view of Northville, photographed from High Rock , shows the Sacandaga River and Northville in the distance. The railroad station is in the lower left corner. A horse-and-buggy ride was always available to and from the station for the many passengers.

The railroad comes to Northville. In 1875, the Fonda, Johnstown, & Gloversville Railroad Company completed a northern extension as far as Northville. This photograph shows one of its early engines, a ten wheeler, being turned on the first turntable, cleverly constructed from steel rail, with Northville and its bridge in the background.

This early photograph shows Northville's first iron bridge, constructed to span the Sacandaga River at Northville. This bridge was built in 1882 to replace a wooden bridge that had washed away earlier that year. No photographs of the first bridge have ever been found.

The Riverside Hotel was located on the north side of Bridge Street, just after it enters the village of Northville. The Riverside was one of the many smaller drinking and boarding establishments that catered to the needs of the summer vacationers and loggers entering Northville after leaving the train station or arriving from points north. The proprietors were C.E. Tunnicliff and Truman Rice.

Patrick H. Conroy's business produced gloves and mittens. Conroy, in the doorway, poses for a photograph with his family and employees at his business on Reed Street during one winter *c.* 1910.

This view of Northville's business district was taken looking south. William Barker's Hard Pan Store, at the left, was built before the Civil War. At the time of the photograph, this location had been acquired by L.N. Johnson, who owned the Hard Pan Store until it closed in 1917. After that, the building was used as a movie house known as the Star Theater and operated until the late 1960s. After that, various businesses occupied the location and today, the Plugs Plus auto parts store makes use of the aging wooden structure. The wooden building attached to the Hard Pan Store was a hardware store and the small wooden structure to its south was a butcher shop.

Cam Checquer ran a blacksmith shop on the first floor of this building. At the time this photograph was taken, a wagon repair shop, operated by Gus Elsinor, was in business on the second floor. This structure, located on the southeastern corner of Bridge and First Streets, also housed a shoe store, owned and operated by Leslie Sweet and his wife, Mary Sweet, from 1918 until the early 1970s. Today, this structure has been renovated by artist Anne Miller for use as a residence and the Common Ground Gallery.

At the Northville Station c. 1895, a horse-drawn hack operated by the Osborn Inn in Newtons Corners has just loaded passengers and hunting gear that are headed for the inn. The four-horse Tally Ho stage, on the right, carries the rest of the hunting party headed for the north woods. Notice the men posing with their oil-cloth encased hunting rifles.

The large two-story Union Free School was built on the east side of South Main Street in 1888 to meet the educational needs of the village's increasing population. Grades one through eight were taught here until the current Northville School was constructed on South Third Street in 1933. This photograph shows the front of the old school and an addition that was built on the back in 1920. Classes have been suspended for what is believed to be a trip to the village cemeteries on Memorial Day to place flags on the veterans' graves.

With reins in hand, driver Jack Green holds the stage nicknamed the Tally Ho in front of the Northville House, located on the west side of North Main Street. These men and their dogs were photographed in 1895 on their way north for a hunting trip.

This hunting party heads to the Adirondacks in the Tally Ho stage, which makes a stop at Uriah Patrick's home on North Main Street. Patrick, seated with his dog on the porch, was a member of the Northville Rod and Gun Club, which used lands near Lake Pleasant and Piseco for hunting excursions. Patrick's house still stands and is now the Adirondack Country Store. Opened in 1988 by Joyce Teshoney, the store is filled to capacity with Adirondack furnishings and has a good selection of books pertaining to the Adirondack region.

Ray Hubbell was one of Northville's early entrepreneurs. The upper photograph shows Hubbell's first factory on North Second Street. It was established in 1880 for the production of his patented metal corners for tablecloths and floor covering made from oilcloth. This site burned in 1890 and a second factory was built. Various partnerships and manufacturing businesses were ventured by Hubbell throughout the village. The photograph below shows Hubbell in his sleigh in front of his home on the northeast corner of Third and Bridge Streets, near the beginning of the 20th century. The man of the left appears to be the postman who kept the mail moving through the snow.

Hubbell's Bridge St. Northville N. Y.

No space was wasted here. In 1875, Edwin Allen and Andrew Palmer teamed up to buy Samuel B. Benton's hardware business, built on North Main Street next to the Hard Pan Store in 1870. The Allen and Palmer Hardware Store carried everything from guns and sporting goods to wood stoves and furnaces. The store was moved to its present location at 112 North Main Street in 1969 by William Conover, who took over the store in 1960 and supervised its operation until 1997. Today, Shawn Darling and his partner Leland Robinson Jr. own and operate the Allen and Palmer Store, now nearing its 125th year of business. The store's original location was used for a short time as a bicycle shop. Then, in 1977, Russ Gleaves, a musician and dealer of rare books and antiquities, reopened the doors of the old building as an antique shop. Today, Gleaves and his sons Tom and Russ Jr. maintain the antique store.

In 1930, the new Northville Bridge, built to span the Sacandaga Reservoir, looms over the old iron bridge that served the village for almost 50 years. One of the iron placards visible atop the old bridge was found recently by scuba divers and can be seen at the Northampton Museum located on Northville's South Main Street. The structure to the right was the Riverview Hotel.

This photograph of Fish Rock Cut was taken during road construction on the highway leaving Northville heading toward Hope Falls. The old Hudson auto was purchased by the laborers for runs into town. A labor dispute brought work to a halt, and the contractor cut wages in half. That evening, the laborers headed to one of the blacksmith shops in town and, one by one, had their shovels cut in half down the middle. The contractor soon reinstated full wages, and construction recommenced.

The religious encampment at the Circle was established across the river just south of the village of Northville sometime after the Civil War. Originally begun by the Methodists, this area was a popular wilderness meeting ground for revivals and Bible studies long before the railroad to Northville was built. After the railroad arrived, most of the land along the west bank of the river was purchased. The Adirondack Conferences Circle in the woods soon gave way to wooden benches and a small pavilion; the tents soon gave way to small wooden cottages built around the Circle. As the park grew to massive proportions, ultimately encompassing the meeting grounds, the religious groups decided that a quieter meeting place was needed. They reportedly established a new location near Round Lake.

A large group of sojourners, possibly from one of the local glove shops, poses for a photograph on the north side of the first station at Sacandaga Park.

This photograph was taken soon after the Adirondack Inn at Sacandaga Park was first built. Two additions in the 1890s almost doubled the inn's size. An impressive structure, the Adirondack Inn was unoccupied for a short time before it was destroyed by fire in 1975.

This photograph captures a view from Riverside Boulevard, looking west of the entrance to the Sacandaga Park midway and its many attractions. Notice the old Stanley Steamer on the right.

These people pose for a picture at the park. The miniature steam engine named Sacandaga was a popular attraction at the park and a great prop for a picture postcard memento from Sacandaga Park.

106

Sport Island at Sacandaga Park hosted many events during the summers. In this photograph, the miniature steam train carries passengers out to the island past a military encampment, believed to be that of Company B from Cohoes.

Capt. Thomas Sackett Baldwin and his Red Devil biplane thrill the crowds on Sport Island. Baldwin was a true pioneer of aviation. In 1904, he built and flew the first American dirigible, the California Arrow. As a friend of Glenn Curtis of the Curtis Aeroplane Company, Baldwin built his Red Devil pusher biplane using the Curtis pattern in 1910. Baldwin had been thrilling crowds worldwide for many years and was in the area during the summer of 1913 when this photograph was taken at Sacandaga Park.

Stuart Wilson, who became known as the "Sacandaga hermit," moved to the park from nearby Gloversville sometime near the end of the 19th century. Wilson built a ramshackle hut west of the first railroad station in what was an unused portion of the park. A photographer in earlier years, Wilson set up an old camera at his shack in the woods. Many of the sojourners visiting the park traveled along the narrow path to Wilson's for a 5¢ tintype portrait, considered old-fashioned by this time, as a memento from the park. Wilson is shown in the tintype self-portrait on the left.

In 1920, Sacandaga Park got a new station, located approximately 400 feet north of the old station, which had occupied the southeastern corner lot where the railroad crossed Lincoln Avenue. The post office was relocated here and continued service until 1967. This station is one of the few remaining structures from the old railroad that still exist today. In recent years, artisan Lawrence Faust remodeled the old station into a working studio apartment and transformed the lawn, once the main entrance to the park, into an outdoor gallery for his many sculpted creations. This picture was taken in 1922. In this crowd of people were the stockholders of the Fonda, Johnstown, & Gloversville Railroad, on a trip with the new gas car No. 200, which is sitting on the tracks in front of the station.

Built in 1901 on a high bluff overlooking the Sacandaga Valley from the west, High Rock Lodge was named for a large boulder that was a favorite destination for many travelers. High Rock boasted lush gardens, romantic wooded paths, tennis courts, horse stables, riding trails, and a beautiful view from each of the front-facing rooms. The lodge was a popular destination and continued to operate until its destruction by fire in 1951.

High Rock 2000 ft. above sea level, Sacandaga Park, N. Y.

The trail to High Rock was a short but steep walk from Sacandaga Park. Many postcards were made and photographs were taken showing families, friends, and young lovers enjoying the view from here.

No 626. A Train load of Logs, Northville, N. Y.

A load of maple logs heads out of Northville, on its way to by rail to the highest bidding veneer mill, operated by Mr. Hartwell, who had leased John A. Willard's sawmill. Hartwell often sold on consignment the best veneer timber for the local lumbermen.

Gifford's Corners School was built in 1904 to replace a small one-room school located on the southwestern corner of the intersection of Mountain Road and the old road to Gloversville, just below the southern entrance to Sacandaga Park. The roadbed of the Fonda, Johnstown, & Gloversville Railroad ran directly behind the schoolhouse, which must have delighted many schoolchildren as class was interrupted each day by the loud steam engine and its whistle signaling the road crossing.

Osborns Covered Bridge was built in 1840 to replace a floating bridge built *c*. 1920 by Calvin Osborn, one of the earliest settlers in the area and the source of both the bridge's name and in 1831, the settlement's name. The new single-lane bridge was over 250 feet in length with only one center abutment and used a simple but sturdy cross-braced timber design. During a heavy spring freshet from the Adirondacks in 1859, the waters of the Sacandaga pushed the bridge off its high piers. The bridge separated in the center and its two halves ended up resting on opposite shores just downstream. Due to its sturdy construction, the bridge was reassembled on presumably slightly higher piers.

This early homestead was lost to the lake. The home and its impressive windmill were built by S.R. Partridge of Osborns Bridge. Partridge and his wife are enjoying a game of croquet on the front lawn, as the family dog looks on from under the shade tree to the right.

This early photo postcard speaks for itself. Engine No. 8 has just arrived at the Cranberry Creek Station on a run to Northville. This station and the rail bed were lost to the lake in 1930.

Before the arrival of the Sacandaga Reservoir, most of the hamlet of Cranberry Creek was built within the town of Northampton. After the lake covered most of this settlement, what remained became part of the western shoreline, still within the boundary of the town of Mayfield.

This small boarding establishment, known as Fricks Hotel, was Cranberry Creek's largest hotel.

This photograph shows the Lewis C. Smith home and business. This location served the hamlet of Cranberry Creek for many years as a general store, blacksmith shop, glove shop, post office, and in later years, as a regular stop for automobiles headed in and out of the Sacandaga Valley in need of gasoline or service. Smith was also a justice of the peace; thus, it is presumed that some marriage ceremonies were performed here.

Completed in 1818, the Fish House Covered Bridge was considered the best-designed and best-constructed bridge in upstate New York. This massive 380-foot-long double-lane structure was built utilizing spanning arches cut from solid timbers, each over 100 feet in length. No one is quite sure whether the timbers were bent while still green or after being steamed. None the less, this bridge stood for 112 years and was still in excellent condition when, with the other structures built in the Sacandaga Valley, it succumbed to the rising waters of the reservoir.

This photograph shows the interior of the two-lane bridge at Fish House. It gives an idea of the size of the solid, arched support timbers and the overall construction design of the bridge.

The Fish House Hotel was a landmark to the residents of Northampton. Built in 1802, it stood on the village square, where five roads from all corners of the Sacandaga Valley intersected. Mr. Kelly, on the porch, was the proprietor at the time of this photograph, c. 1900.

This is where Sacandaga Valley children learned their three R's. This school at Northampton, now called the Fish House, today serves as a community hall.

This was one of the many beautiful homes in the community of Northampton. Originally built by Dr. Langdon Marvin and his wife, Lucy Beecher, the house was later occupied by their daughter Lucy and her husband, Frank Sinclair. The Sinclair family are shown on the porch in this photograph taken c. 1900. In an area that later became a large garden, Sir William Johnson had built a small log fishing and hunting camp in 1762, which he named Fish House Lodge. Johnson was considered by many as the most influential man in North America at that time. The community of Northampton was always nicknamed Fish House by the area residents and, in 1961, its citizens persuaded the State of New York to officially change its name to Fish House.

118

John A. Willard's lumber mill was located on the west bank of the Sacandaga River, within the Fonda, Johnstown, & Gloversville Railroad freight yard and behind the Northville Station. This was the first large mill along the Sacandaga and often gathered some of the best logs for sawing or veneer. Later, a veneer mill was built in the hamlet of Wells to compete for this valuable timber.

This tar paper-covered log camp was typical of lumber camps in the Adirondacks. Located in Hope Falls, the camp is identified as one that was operated by John A. Willard of Northville.

These men keep the timber moving as the individual logs spill over one of the small dams constructed on each side of Sport Island.

Crews were assigned sections of the river to keep watch for logjams. This crew with peaveys in hand was photographed near Parkville. Second from the right is Roy Cunningham. His wife, Edith Cunningham, was a grade-school teacher and one of the village's early historians.

At this time, Colonel Hartwell had leased the John A. Willard Sawmill. Hartwell, in the center with his hands in his pockets and wearing a black derby hat and coat, stopped production for a short time to be photographed with his crew.

Giant pine logs head to market. This was a typical scene throughout the north woods in winter. After the trees were cut, they were dragged to a landing, such as this one, where a team of horses or oxen was hitched to a large sleigh. The sleigh was then loaded for the trip to a nearby river or lumber mill or to a larger landing near a railroad. Sadly, many of these work animals and their drivers were killed when heavy loads went out of control while heading down a hill.

Teams of oxen gathered at the Northville freight yards. These oxen were photographed presumably for a winter parade in town. Like horses, the oxen were used extensively by the local lumbermen to skid huge loads of logs to the sawmills throughout the winter. A good team of oxen was a great source of pride within this competitive industry.

These two photographs show local lumbermen at work near Northville c. 1900. In the top photograph, Seymour Willard, son of John A. Willard, is seated on a log being cut to length with a two-man bucksaw. The man on the right is Carl Harvey. In the bottom photograph, Seymour Willard, near the door of a small work camp, looks on as the crew prepares for a day's work.

The Sacandaga Boom Company constructed stone-filled cribbing near the bend in the Sacandaga River, below Osborn Bridge, to aid the lumbermen in controlling the flow of logs headed for the Hudson.

The early postcard from the town of Day in Saratoga County mistakenly identifies this scene as a logjam. Throughout the winter, logs were often stacked along riverbanks. In the spring, the rising waters from the spring freshets floated the logs down the river way to the large paper mills and sawmills at Corinth and Glens Falls.

In the spring of 1930, in front of what was known for many years as the Tamarack Tavern, the Hudson River Regulating District's workboat the *Mystic II* is ready to be backed down the hill on Riverside Boulevard into the waters of the Sacandaga Reservoir.

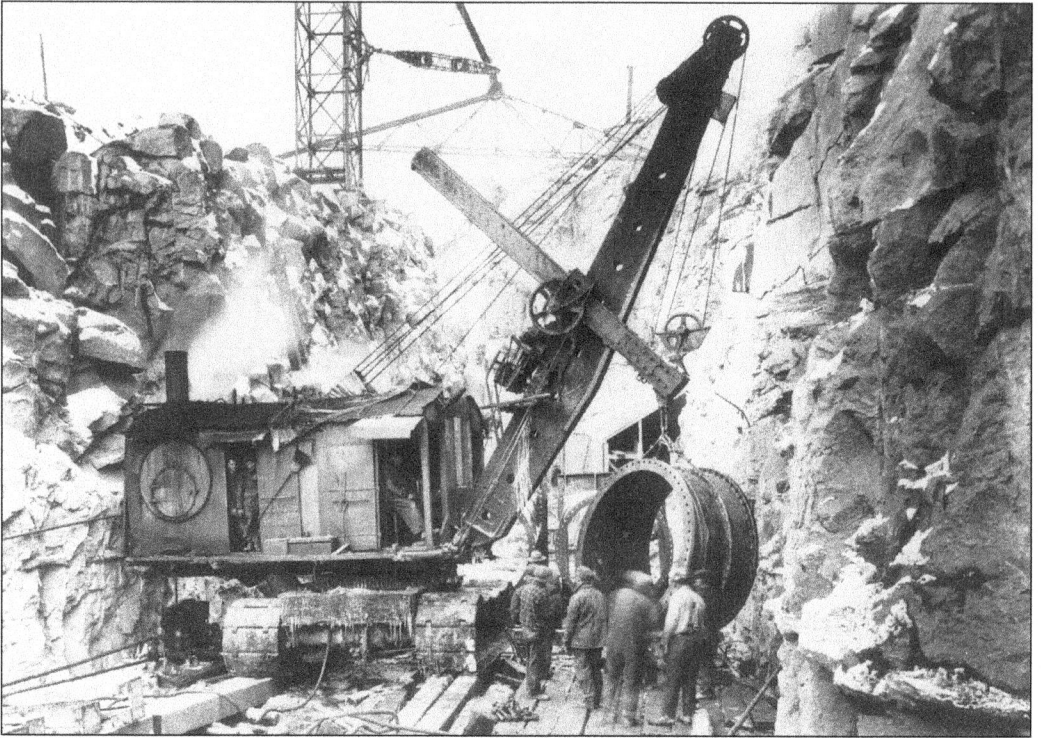

These two photographs show the earthen dam project at Conklingville under construction in 1929. The upper photograph shows the heavy equipment used during the placement of steel linings for the control valves that regulate the waters of the Sacandaga. In the lower photograph, some of the Sacandaga River Valley as well as the three-span iron bridge and the village of Conklingville, which it served, are visible in the distance.

This panoramic postcard was made shortly after the Sacandaga Valley was flooded with an estimated 280 billion gallons of water, as three 9-foot-diameter valves were closed, forcing the Sacandaga River to flood the valley that it had given life to for ages. Lost to the lake, completely or in part, were the settlements of Parkville, Osborns Bridge, Cranberry Creek, Munsonville, Benedict, North Broadalbin, Northampton (later named Fish House), Batchellerville, Beechers Hollow, West Day, Day Center, and Conklingville. Gone too is Sport Island and the midway at Sacandaga Park, as well as the railroad that survived in large part from the summer tourist trade generated here. The trade-off for this loss was considered quite a success. No longer did the businesses and communities along the Hudson River Valley have to suffer the devastating monetary losses from the yearly flooding nor endure the physical hardships of the epidemics that often followed from the residual mud, refuse, and silt that remained long after the waters had subsided. The dam also continues to generate power, helping to satisfy the ever increasing needs for electricity. The raging debates concerning the fate of the valley have long since past, and the Hudson River Regulating Dam remains a testament to the indefatigable pursuit of the betterment of mankind.

The Following
RULES and REGULATIONS

Are maintained to the strictest degree.
All who patronize this Beach may benefit
equally and without any partiality.

---

1. Bathers using this Beach do so at their own risk.
2. A lifeguard shall be provided and shall be on duty from 10:30 to 6 p.m. July 1st to Sept 3d.
3. The lifeguard boat is to be used by no one except the lifeguard.
4. There is to be no ball playing on the Beach.
5. There shall be no disrobing on the Beach, either by Adults or Children.
6. No dogs are permitted on the Beach.
7. There is to be no parking of automobiles between the Beach and the road.
8. Lessons by the lifeguard will be given before 11 a.m., between 12 and 1:30 p.m. and after 6 p.m.
9. Refuse barrels are provided and all bottles, papers, and refuse of any kind must be put in same by user.
10. There are to be no Hawkers or Peddlers of any kind permitted on the Beach or in the area adjacent.

Jack McDowell
Deputy Sheriff, Saratoga Park

These photographs were taken during the first year of the lake's creation in 1930. The beach goers near Northville, in the above photograph, had to follow these ten rules and regulations, which were posted at the entrance. The new beach is shown in the photograph below. Since the lake's formation, the beaches and the communities along its shores have become a favorite destination for tourists and many area residents.

128